Open Letters To The Sky

Bren Booth-Jones

First published 2022 by The Hedgehog Poetry Press

Published in the UK by
The Hedgehog Poetry Press
5, Coppack House
Churchill Avenue
Clevedon
BS21 6QW

www.hedgehogpress.co.uk

ISBN: 978-1-913499-79-2

9 8 7 6 5 4 3 2 1

A CIP Catalogue record for this book is available from the British Library.

For Mom & Dad

All the fictional in these characters are poems.

To whom should I address this letter?

—Jessica Lightfoot-Toye

Contents

DEAR READER

—After James Tate

Hi. How are you?

I write this line sitting at my desk, thinking pale echoes
to float through your mind's garden.

Can you see the crescent scar
rising over the hedge of my brow
where the moon tried to eat me?

I try to see you too.

I almost catch the cadence of your voice

in the car's headlights that wash
yellow and lonesome

across my curtains,
over my desk, over the blurred polaroid
of you in the cemetery holding a snake.

Or is it a lace? Is it a garden? Is it me?
I'm sorry, it's not me, it's you, holding the line.
It's not a garden, it's a hospital carpark. It's raining.

Lightning fizzles down the spine of the night
like a shiver.

Rain shatters the river. But it's not a river it's a road,

wind laughing in the trees along it.
I send letters like pale moths on the wind.

Moths like flickering telegrams

addressed to you and you and you.

To you, locked
in the coral heart of the moon.

But I have no flaming snowflake
to unlatch the door to that planetarium.

What to do?

The night fades. It's morning. No,

it's afternoon. I'm in the cemetery.
The sun searches a stack of clouds
for misplaced records

and a white-bearded man
bends painfully to place a daisy on a grave.

He closes his eyes and remembers the spring morning
yesterday, no, 70 years ago,

when he first saw her, his Annie--

and what a speed-blur procession followed!
Exams trenches placenta
penny farthings industrial farming
fright and joy
disappointment
nicotine machines medals
lust loss coffins longing
grit pride boredom. Bacteria. Antibiotics.

Reverie.
                    Her face in light and shadow.

Now he turns
in the watered-down sun
and opens his eyes, looks straight at me, through me,
up and out of the poem, over

my pen, over the skyline, up
into the rush of blue

that bruises and bruises into black galaxies
faster and faster
all the way back in lap
after lap round the sun
and into a white blinding flash
and a telegram says

DEAREST, I'LL WAIT FOR YOU

POSTE RESTANTE 1

Poste Restante is a service designed for travellers who do not have a permanent address in the location where they wish to receive mail...

—postoffice.co.uk

DEAR AMSTERDAM

—For Mark Davidson

I'm walking home beneath an autumn sky
the shattered blue of a drunken dawn.

Clouds freshly painted are at risk of running
over rooftops, awnings, bridges, canals,
a sky speckled with swallows. A distant shout.

I see and hear many strange and sparkling things:

artisanal cheese, artisanal weed,
a phone repair shop with a sign saying,
    DON'T WORRY IT'S ONLY BROKEN.

"Our sons will surely grow up to be
the kind of mothers
our fathers never were"

"Remember to keep 1.5 metres distance from yourself"

Ahead is the park, a green and yellow shimmer

that soon swallows me. I pass yoga classes
and designer dogs, trees of medieval gold and red.

And then I see my neighbour,
the Somalian architect,
teaching his precocious kid

taekwondo.

In a nearby stanza
his Irish wife hurls red paint at a white canvas.

Beyond the park, the bridge flows over the river,
the river flows over stylised bones and radical slime,
the ribcage of a shopping trolley,
a doll's head with one blue eye.

Then, following myself home,
as fish choke on household names,
the bridge melts into my street

and the river says to me, in a crystal whisper,
Everything is incomplete. Haunted. Mosaic.

The Amstel River slithers through this half-built heaven

and I pass an ice cream smeared into the road
with a crow flapping over it, sugar-smashed,
banquet of ecstasy--
and its blue-black beak is a brush dipped in paint.

And my heart is the same: always seeking
someone else's wasted sweetness.

And the river says, *Brendon! You keep riding your luck!
But to where? To where?*

NOTE SCRIBBLED ON A VAN GOGH CALENDAR

—For Mathieu & Rachel

Why did your heart schedule me for December?
—Noir Disco

Calendar above my bed:
May: the harsh grid of days
softened by luminous
blue-white roses so close to wilting—

how the agony of being
is seared
into every brushstroke—

the sad angles of the leaves
seasick green in mossy light

at the asylum in May 1890—

and here I lay
130 years gone
with the click of a mouse
and time still ripping pages off the wall
rapid as ever
rabid rush

yet each fresh month
brings me an attempt to capture
your attempts to capture
life in quivering colour—

how silly my little chores
across the grid of days!

reregister date with X pushups don't smoke submit assignment buy
painkillers don't smoke submit this poem run shop make up with Y
clean up calm down don't stop

and above it all, your serene roses

knowing your body was nearly burned up—
knowing you would be forgotten
before you were even remembered—

LETTER TO THE SKY

—*In memory of Adel Beres*

Please. Don't talk to me
about god's doting microscope of love.

Where is Adel's lazy guardian angel
on her long walk, sunstruck and reeling,
to this drunk city's heartless outer limit?

To the quiet industrial deadzone
where two centuries of screeching cows
were milked to death
for little squares of airbrushed cheese.

Can you hear the haunted breath,
the walls that don't forget, the walls that see and see?

Now only broken glass, weeds, junk metal, graffiti, ruin.

Train tracks curve away to their vanishing point.

Sunlight and dust and forgetting. Rusted desolation.

Where the dove's wing, where the love?
Your tears run and run and splash
your knuckles gripping the rail. Adel, your tears disappear on impact,
annihilated by the sun--

over the abandoned factories, the sky of illusory blue--

behind the sky, racing cosmic depths.

The train grows louder and you brace your every atom,
limbs shaking, waiting, waiting
for the steel spikes in your heart to stop stabbing.

Not one angel comes for you.

Not one fucking angel

to say, *Adel, don't let your iridescence die!*
To hold you back and stroke your hurt away.
To tell you of your immeasurable beauty and worth!

Oh Adel! Is god mad, dead or indifferent?

My question is met with predictable silence,
the blue sky blank as a turned back.

Adel, please turn back.

I should have checked in more often. What
uselessness:
I should have:
you can't put your arms around an elegy.

The last time I saw you. Nightclub. Blue strobe.
And your green quiet intense eyes said,
I've been out to the far edge of my inner orbit.
And I said, *You dredged deep swing into your syntax.*

But why didn't I ask if you'd left some heat behind,
or what it cost you to live in ellipsis?

Adel. There is no hand of grace
to turn the rage
of corrosive chemicals in your brain
back into their gentler elements.

You stand brave on the rail over the tracks.

Forever 21.

The train is hurtling like a curse.

You face the universe. Green eyes brave.

All I can do is stop writing what comes next.

All I can say is this:

Dearest Adel. The end of heartache.

Adel, Adel, Adel!

LETTER COMPOSED FROM CIGARETTE BUTTS

—For Nigel Kent

All the cigs I smoked. Toked skunk. Sunk beers. Bear roars in hung over
head. Heart scars, heat scars. Star dust sentience. Sentence of endless
petals. Dental bills threatened. Thread unravelled. Rattle cough. Cost of
habits. Habitat collapsing. Six hundred letters never sent. Scent of fragrant
summer rain. Range of mountains. Maintained composure. Postured
confidence. Confined pattern. Patent expired. Expressed desire. Mortal
moon. Bloom soon.

POSTE RESTANTE 2

In your next letter I wish you'd say
where you are going and what you are doing;
how are the plays, and after the plays
what other pleasures you're pursuing:
taking cabs in the middle of the night,
driving as if to save your soul...

—Elizabeth Bishop

DEAR HYPOTHETICAL LOVER

I

Will I ever earn enough
to not have the recurring dream

every night for a week
before payday
of the rat-eaten piggy bank,

the wolf with his bacon breath
sitting on my chest
like a diamond-bellied Buddha,

the nightclub bouncer guarding the chi
of despotic toddlers with sticky fingers
on atomic weaponry

Can't they see I'm trying?

How deep must I swim to recover
the black box from the wreck?

It's true, I've been a fucking mess.

Everything is screaming, *Forget.*

I need leave to remain.

I've got beef with death--

II

But you and I,
we're done
living bloodless as crockery.

Let's share our electrons and spend
each day in a sonnet, each
night in a starlit lexicon.

Let's live together
in a mood of the bluest orange
and read

the palm of every fallen leaf.

And to the world we'll be stranger
than a trilobite in a trilby,

but we won't care.

Our souls were akimbo
in the vomitorium too long. Too long.

III

So now the question is:

how to enter this
different kind of knowing,
this different way
of attending?

This meaning
is always in motion.

It's true, I've been a fucking mess.
But now I know

that all phenomena interlock.
Ion. Embryo. Amaryllis.

The mint between the concrete's teeth.

Carapace. Ejecta. Alligator.

I'm working to be better,
to replace this PTSD with sleep,

to be weightless when you're with me.

PLEASE FIND ATTACHMENT

—For Anneloes

Please find attached the faded snapshot of 14 year old me at the church party awkwardly holding a paper plate of cake and crisps. In the background some ginger kid goes berserk at a piñata. Please note the pose, the flip phone in my pudgy white paw, purple nails, face trying to comb back with a smile the resentment like a painful burp stuck inside me, like a cartoon character that runs and runs but can't escape the raincloud hovering above him. Can't skedaddle. Overdue for puberty. Oversized blazer with the frayed sleeves. Overblown fake gold earrings: little cheap bells chiming *Virgin! Virgin! Virgin!* You can't see the Tamagotchi shitting itself in my pocket, but can you see the way I'm trying and failing to pronounce my own pain, the way I'm trying and failing to look more useful than a vacuum cleaner on a beach? I was held back a year in kindergarten because I couldn't close a circle. Still can't. Tamagotchis were already obsolete when I was 14, but so were poems. And yet here I am writing you to ask if the U.N. might be hiring any poets. Back then, I wanted the world to be my United Sates of Whatever, a trembling cereal isle of loud colour sugar rush that never runs out. I wanted my life to smell of new clothes. Everything was screaming, *Make it through.* Oblivious to all the doors my skin opened, please note the desperate angle of my neck, like peering over a hedge to see the world beyond the thick white scriptural bubble, the clotted cream manicured sepulchral mantra of believe or burn, of turn the other cheek. Or just keep turning.

DEAR DIARY

—For Tiziana

Today was the colour of insurance fine print, dull and deadly. I was running late, as usual, for the last train to the end of history. Late for the latest show-stopping apocalypse. Late for my trip to see X, who lives on the knife-edge of town. Buses crammed the roads like drunk men at a urinal. She saw me trudging over the horizon like the pigeon-toed oaf I am, with my head full of glossy molecules and my face unlayered in joy to see her. She stabbed out her spliff, swished her dark hair, straightened her septum ring. Then she explained what she did to me. As in fight neofeudalism. As in send my heart summersaulting.

We walked to a pretentious café nearby and sat at a wobbly table on the terrace. We talked about the swans in her canal who sail under the walkway to gobble spiders in the dank and gurgling shadows. She said, *Without you the days drag forever and the years blink away in an hour.* I said, *Dip your bucket into the flow of me whenever.* So we agreed to abolish time. I stood up and walked inside.

"Kids" by MGMT was playing. The baristas wore neck tattoos and gentle sneers. This was the kind of café where there is an inverse relationship between the quality of the coffee and the comfort of the seating. As in, *Drink our delicious flat white and then fuck off you intolerable hipster.*

Postmodern cave paintings dripped in violent red silence on the inside of the café's toilet door. *FUKC* and *WHAT IS A POEM?* I sat on the porcelain throne and asked what a poem might be. I remembered the house party where I first met X, techno music losing its mind from a hidden speaker. She looked up from a horizontal mirror speckled in snow and said, *Every line is an air-strike against memory.*

I don't know what a poem is. Can a poem say hurry on back to where she sits waiting on the terrace beyond which rainclouds and grim pigeons tar the day with grimy feathers. Can a poem be an airstrike against forgetting? Can a poem contain this crashy feeling of too much caffeine, too little time, the haunting of white space. Bren. Your coffee's getting cold. But can a poem say, *I wasn't born yesterday. I was born tomorrow.*

EPISTLE

—For Ankh Spice

& you walk through the forest
& your mind links each line
      along a faint green leaf
& *these branches are all the arms we need*
& the undergrowth teems
& a voice is a river of green ages
      of moss & rock & soil
& everything is dreaming
& each bird sips its own reflection
      with no concern
        for time spilling from its heart

DEAR HYPOTHETICAL LOVER

I am out on my Sunday morning walk,
creaking through crisp winter light.
Amsterdam is slowly sinking. I think of you.
How could I not be at least a little in love with you
every time you turn your radiance my way?
But that's my secret. That's between me
and these stately sinking overpriced houses.
How they tip slowly over,
a few inches every year,
to catch a glimpse of themselves
through the mist dissolving on the jade canals,
in whose guts rust bicycles,
machineguns and prams.
But it was worth swallowing that junk, think the canals,
spilling drunkenly into each other,
Worth refashioning what is abandoned
and giving it a home inside yourself.
Like writing poems, like making yourself a poem,
to flow over and through
what is cast into you, what you encase,
voice and haunt, lace
of senses, wheels and handles to steer
the channels of being,
which are the channels of becoming.
Now men in migraine-orange overalls are coming
to sweep Saturday night's broken bottles
and squished fries out of sight.
Broken promises fester better in the dark
below the streets--

but if only you knew how long I really spent
on the playlist I made you!
If only you knew how many times
I've played the imagined movie of our lives
in my head.
And even the endless, cheesy,
made-for-TV sequels
the world cares less and less about--
I have them taped on dusty VHS
in the attic of my brain.
I try not to imagine the final monologue, though,
some black-clad actor alone on a stage
in some tiny modernist theatre,
saying, *If only if only if only*

POSTE RESTANTE 3

In the dream where I first wrote to you, I was worried the letter would get lost. Poetry can be like that: handwritten love letters that arrive sixty years after the war. Which war, you ask?
—Laura Wetherington

NOTE TO SELF (AN EXALTATION OF LARKS)

—For Laura & Martin

Clean your place. Get new shoes. Get new sheets.
Calm down. Buck up. Work out.
Google the capital of Andorra. Floss more.
Google animal collective nouns. Tell them about
a crash of rhinos. A kaleidoscope of butterflies.
Talk about episteme. Talk about dark ecology.
Don't talk about your book deal.
Get a better brain. Ask dazzling questions.
Grow three inches taller. Three years younger.
Lose the chin. The stink of loneliness.
Don't be so fucking vampirish.
Get a tan. Thicken beard. Swell bank account.
Don't freak out. Sit up straight. Here they come—

OPEN LETTER TO THE SKY

--For Noir Disco

On the busy street this afternoon
the homeless man is washed in Rembrandt light
and asking for change. And nobody sees.
Swipe left to delete.
But every grog-blossom is a microcosm.

In the twilit trees that line the highway
the birdsong is depleted. But at least I was retweeted.

I'm sorry, but I just need a little bit of outer space.
I'm sorry. I tried to throw myself away.
But there is no away.
There is no cosmic microwave dinner.

Beloved poets, you must change the light.
And you do, you do.
I never thought I'd miss the days before I met you,
and I don't.

Beloved poets, how your music
bootlegs the breeze!
How I'm strung out on flowers when I breathe
your electric etceteras.
Your spiral galaxies of why:
my shaking, calloused hand to hold the book,
to open letter after letter to the sky.

PRESCRIPTION (OR FAREWELL TO A HYPOTHETICAL LOVER)

The doctor says no more doses of you.

Like having no more smokes to bookend the day,
little tiki torches on either side of a gate
to the garden of garrulous glare.

Goodbye to the soporific haze of your jasmine breath
on my neck at midnight.
Goodbye sleep's deep anesthetic.
Now the calendar's sharkskin walls
are suspended between awake and a wake,
wave after wave, blank page,
a stage prop to some awful play
in which Hamlet gives up
language for interpretative dance.

Like I have to give you up.
Like having no more after-work whiskey to pare
the thorns from the pain when I think of you
and what might have been.
This means that until now a certain sharpness
                could cancel a certain sharpness—

two knives forming a gleaming deadly X—
but where do the banished blades disappear to, love?

Answer: the liver,
trout-speckled and too tired
of swimming up-river. Turning in rebellion
towards the devouring mouth of the sea.

Now my liver will be left to pulse
in its dark red compartment
and the thorns of *if only* and *lonely*
must lodge and be broken

down by enzymes and absorbed, circulate for sixty years
in blood and muscle. Some tiny parochial
speck grizzled in the sinew,
or a sprawling cosmopolis
rotting the tissue of the body's map?
Or merely some nocturnal comma notched
in my heart's manuscript?
"Only time will tell if time will tell," wrote Ben Lerner
in a poem I can no longer read you.

And no more pleasure pills to frame the story
in a halcyon halo,
no more botox to pump plumpness
into the slashed tires of mornings without you,
no you to tell me that this poem is taking an overwrought turn, to tell me
what a melodramatic
metaphor *slashed tires* is,
and so it's splashed here, rich and cancerous,
strawberry milkshake spilled
over cigarette butts against the curb,

but no Spacecake Saturday Spooning
to melt glaring headlines
into ambient songs of you
smiling into your diary, you kickboxing
the less-than-brilliant day
into a million glittering pieces,
you capturing Manchester in polaroid
to send me a wedge of water, sky, some warehouse
looking always, through your eyes, somehow Transylvanian—

now the bright blare of voices
rushes inwards, and yours no longer
cutting clear through the muck.
Getting clean sucks. River
and sea collide endlessly.
And the thorns that prick me when I think of you?
Will they ever fade to blue?

DEAR VINCENT VAN GOGH

—For Marina

I get to December besmirched & punctured by dark frosts of longing for a little light. Your calendar is still up on the wall, but so is your time. No longer your mad red one-eared face in these cobbled streets smelling of fish and flowers.

All that time your canvases were covered, till you returned to favour, till your sunflowers & starry swirls unfurled into a million museums

to be coughed on by tremulous dusty dames in black and fidgety ice cream-fingered kids. To be pumped into trinkets, mugs, whistles, USB sticks. And this calendar reminding me of your sorrowful glowing furious conduit of colour.

Dear Van Gogh, you may be boxed and commodified, your body branded, spun to ash. But your force is not vanquished. You slip out of time into yellow fields of shining shifting wheat, a voice from beyond the frame saying, *This is what will remain of us, this quest to express. A voice out of dust. Rusted heart. Star incarnate.*

INDEX

Dear Reader,
Please find attached
the radical Tamagotchi
designed for travelers
of artisanal
haunting.

Dear December,
In your next letter,
your music
on its dazzling
bicycle.
Your mind
on the postmodern
coffee.
Your sunstruck
and vampirish liver.
I am X
in the luminous dreaming.
Let's not talk about
a rat-eaten hypothetical sentience.
But why am I
a wreck?

Dear Adel,
please find attached
my crashy ghost flower
for the starlit birdsong
of you.

ABOUT BREN BOOTH-JONES

Bren Booth-Jones is an Amsterdam-based poet and the author of *Vertigo to Go*, which won the White Label Trois Competition.

ACKNOWLEDGEMENTS

Thank you to the following journals for publishing some of these poems in earlier forms:

As It Ought To Be, Botsotso, Dreich, Feral, The Night Heron Barks, Odd Magazine, Outcast Press, Redivider, Verdancies.

"Open Letter to the Sky (For Adel)" was the winner of the Outcast Press Vol. 6

© Cover designed by Tess Saunders (with the use of an image belonging to Elvis Schmoulianoff)
© Author photo by Ella King

Thank you to Mark at Hedgehog for giving me the joy of seeing two books in the world. Thank you to Niall M Oliver, Vic Pickup and Leonie Rowland for the generous blurbs. And thanks also to Laura Wetherington, Jessica Lightfoot-Toye and Noir Disco for permission to use quotes.

Other quotes come from:

Bishop, Elizabeth. "Letter to N.Y.". The Complete Poems 1927-1979 (Farrar, Straus and Giroux 2004)
Lerner, Ben. The Lichtenberg Figures (Copper Canyon Press 2004).

All other allusions, conscious or otherwise, are present in the spirit of intertextual dialogue.

Thank you to my family and friends for all your love.